THE SUCCESSFUL MIDDLE SCHOOL SCHEDULE

ANN MCCARTY PEREZ, EDD

Printed in the United States of America.

ISBN: 9781737444329

Library of Congress Control Number: 2022930157

Acknowledgements

Thank you to the NMSA team who collaborated in 1982 to create *This We Believe*, as it provided the world with a better understanding of the importance of educating young adolescents. In addition, to the AMLE team who continued the work with the fifth edition, *The Successful Middle School: This We Believe*, which gives this book its roots and beginnings. *The Successful Middle School Schedule* is just one piece of the body of work of the Association of Middle Level Education (AMLE) and the dedicated educators that serve young adolescents. Their desire to publish this work and belief in my ability to do so has made this work possible.

Simon Sinek's publication of *Start with Why* provides educators with a framework to understand the why, how, and what of anything we do. The golden circle has highly influenced not only this work, but the work of many learning organizations. When we better understand why we are working on initiatives in our schools, the how and the what become much clearer.

Thank you to my colleagues at Creative Leadership Solutions who have read drafts and provided thoughtful questions and additions to this work. Their insight and experience as authors kept the work moving forward and centered around best practices in education. A special thanks to Doug Reeves, Christine Smith, Nino Collado, and Emily Freeman for multiple reads and coaching sessions.

Throughout my 25 plus years in education, I have served with exceptional administrators and teachers who have provided me with a wealth of understanding and experience on how to best serve students. Coupled with exceptional school staff has been thousands of exceptional students that I have had the honor of serving and learning from.

Lastly, thank you to my family and loving husband Tony who has consistently supported and encouraged me in my educational endeavors.

Contents

SECTION 3: The What
Creating a Responsive Middle School Schedule

Introduction

THE RESEARCH

Since the inception of *This We Believe*, the Association for Middle Level Education's (AMLE) landmark position statement first published in 1982, middle level educators have been reading and studying the characteristics of effective middle grades schools. The document was born from a collective group of educators passionate about the concept that the learning needs of young adolescents were different than high school and elementary students. *This We Believe* quickly became an essential resource for schools that had been trying to implement the middle school model since the 1960s. It provided a true definition of the young adolescent and detailed their unique programming needs. Later, one of the key insights that emerged through the work of Michael Rettig (2000) is that middle school schedules should implement longer and more flexible time blocks to be responsive to and address the developmental needs of the students they serve. In my own research, I found that not only longer and more flexible periods were important, but teacher preparation and appropriate pedagogy also helped define an effective middle school schedule (McCarty, 2010). Most recently, Hebbeln (2021) notes the importance of using the schedule as a tool to address issues brought about by the COVID-19 pandemic. Across time, what we know to be true is that there is great power in the schedule and leaders should use this tool thoughtfully and strategically to best meet the needs of the students they serve. The schedule is one of the most useful and impactful tools that a leader can use to address student needs, implement new initiatives, and drive progress.

Over the past four decades, we have seen the original 14 Characteristics of *This We Believe* grow and evolve to the 18 Characteristics outlined in the 2021 fifth edition, *The Successful Middle School: This We Believe* as we continue to define how to meet the needs of young adolescents. We have studied how the impact of changes in education and the world around us affect programming and offerings in middle school programs. The landscape is complex and those charged with leading schools face many difficult decisions. Perhaps one of the most wide-reaching decisions a school leader makes is that of the schedule. The schedule is a tool leaders can use to design unique and creative programming specific to their school and their students. It is the one thing that truly affects everyone. From start times to end times, it impacts parents, bus drivers, food service staff, teachers, and students. As we approach the schedule, it is not enough to just study the 18 Characteristics. It is our imperative to put them into action. This companion guide to *The Successful Middle School: This We Believe* will help schools explore both the cultural and technical aspects of school scheduling as well as begin to execute the suggested recommendations for programming.

THE SUCCESSFUL MIDDLE SCHOOL: THIS WE BELIEVE

The fifth edition of AMLE's foundational text, *The Successful Middle School: This We Believe* describes the ideal middle grades school as one built around five Essential Attributes "which can be realized and achieved best through the 18 characteristics, which are grouped into three categories – Culture and Community; Curriculum, Instruction and Assessment; and Leadership and Organization" (AMLE, 2021). *The Successful Middle School Schedule* is a companion "field guide" to that text which serves to help middle grades educators explore both the cultural and technical sides of scheduling and how the Essential Attributes and 18 Characteristics offer lenses through which to see your schedule. Ideas and strategies for school schedules are tied to *The Successful Middle School: This We Believe* and linked to research and best practice.

ABOUT THIS BOOK

The Successful Middle School Schedule is organized in three sections. In Section 1, we explore the cultural aspects of middle schools that help build the foundation for a schedule that is as unique as the students it serves. We explore how school culture and shared beliefs can help identify priorities in the schedule and create a driving path tied to the 18 Characteristics of successful middle grades schools. This helps in developing a schedule built on the research and best practices for what we know works in educating young adolescents.

In Section 2, we begin our exploration of the technical aspects of scheduling, providing specific strategies to create a responsive and equitable schedule that reflects the needs of the school's students. This section will include what I call "the deep data dive" which should directly inform your scheduling process. Throughout the data review process, readers are continually encouraged to think about the equity and responsiveness their schedule currently allows and what changes they want to embrace. As in Section 1, Section 2 will explore how specific scheduling strategies are tied to the 18 Characteristics.

In Section 3 we complete the technical side of scheduling, taking teams through specific action steps to create the building blocks for their responsive middle school schedule. This section contains ideas, roles, and reflective questions for teams to consider as they explore all the possibilities that a schedule can offer their school. In this section are sample schedules that include a short description, and the benefits and challenges. I close this section with expert advice, or my favorite rules for scheduling. After creating countless school schedules, these are my favorites and I share them with you to close the book.

This book outlines a recommended process schools can consider before embarking on a schedule change based on both research and practice. It can be used by school communities to help them establish either all or portions of the middle school philosophy and a responsive schedule that embraces the 18 Characteristics and is designed to meet the unique needs of young adolescents.

SECTION 1

The Why: Cultural Aspects of School Schedules

- Vision and Mission
- The Why of Your Schedule
- Belief Statements
- Culture
- Start with a Difficult Conversation
- Collective Responsibility

Some people ask, do you just *see* schedules or what? I say yes and no. What I see is the potential that, with the correct process, harnesses the power to create effective change in schools. The schedule can help us realize best practices and programming that we know to be ideal for our students, staff, and entire learning community.

Figure 1 The Power of Combining Culture and Strategy

The Scheduling Process

VISION/MISSION/VALUES		
DRIVING PATH	CULTURE / STRATEGY	GUIDING PATH
	BELIEF STATEMENTS / DATA REVIEW	
	PRACTICES / PRIORITIES	
	BEHAVIORS / EQUITY	
	ACTION	

In Figure 1 we see the entire process of creating a responsive school schedule from beginning to end, driven by the culture, guided by strategies, and anchored by the vision, mission, and values. Throughout the book, we will dive into each step in this process.

CHAPTER 1: VISION AND MISSION

The Successful Middle School: This We Believe
Characteristics Crossover

- A shared vision developed by all stakeholders guides every decision
- Policies and practices are student-centered, unbiased, and fairly implemented
- Leaders are committed to and knowledgeable about young adolescents, equitable practices, and educational research

Let's begin our journey by reviewing high-level goals and declarations that guide

the work of schools. I'm referring to **vision and mission statements**. To begin the scheduling process, school teams should take time to review their vision and mission statements. This process helps focus the work by identifying larger goals for serving students and developing collective beliefs. When we look at the 18 Characteristics, within Leadership and Organization a, "shared vision developed by all stakeholders guides every decision" is first. *The Successful Middle School: This We Believe* further states that the "school's vision lights the way toward achieving a responsive and equitable education for every young adolescent." The vision encompasses the high-level goals that outline the **why** of our schedules. When we strive to embrace these Essential Attributes in our schedule, a clear vision helps to focus the decisions that we make in terms of time and resources. This aim is further achieved by a clear mission statement.

The mission statement is a school's founding purpose, often seen as a public declaration of commitments and the path for how they will achieve their overarching goals (vision). Mission statements should include action words and phrases that everyone can understand. It serves as the baseline document, informing everyone of daily operations, the underlying value system, and how decisions are made. In middle school vision and mission statements, we strive to include specific wording that acknowledges the uniqueness of the young adolescent while honoring the larger picture of district goals and values. Clarity in our vision and mission helps make decisions for our scheduling easier and more attainable.

Vision and Mission Reflection Exercise

Locate your school vision and mission statements. Place them in the boxes below. Evaluate the text and look for action words. Complete the chart below by entering the statements and answering the questions.

Example

Vision Statement:
Empowering all students to be lifelong learners and responsible citizens

Mission Statement:
We are an inclusive school community committed to academic excellence and integrity. We recognize the needs of young adolescents to be empowered and have a voice in their learning; therefore, we will provide instruction in a caring, safe, and healthy environment responsive to each student in collaboration with families and community.

Action Words	Shared Beliefs or Values	Is There a Why?	Is There a How?	Is There a What?	Language Specific to Young Adolescents
Empower Provide Collaboration	*Students should be empowered, included, and have a voice*	*Students should be lifelong learners and responsible citizens*	*Instruction in a caring, safe, and healthy environment*	*Responsive-ness to each student*	*Yes*

SCHOOL NAME:					
Vision Statement:					
Mission Statement:					
Action Words	Shared Beliefs or Values	Is There a Why?	Is There a How?	Is There a What?	Language Specific to Young Adolescents

Some schools have opted to combine vision and mission or use just one statement. If this is the case, evaluate that single statement using the same questions.

CHAPTER 2: THE WHY OF YOUR SCHEDULE

In education we are often asked "why do we do things?" or "why this initiative and why not that one?" Simon Sinek (2009) outlines the importance of starting with "why" and how the concept changed his thinking forever. Sinek developed the golden circle, which works from the inside out of **why, how, and what**. The golden circle has its roots in the golden ratio/mean. Most of us are familiar with the golden mean as you likely studied it in college—that sweet spot where everything comes together between excess and deficiency (Aristotle). Applying this thinking to scheduling, developing the why behind our master schedules is the first and most important action you will do. A well-established "why" helps scheduling teams determine the elements of their schedule and creates the path for the how and the what. Activities in this book, paired with a thorough review of the 18 Characteristics of successful middle grades schools will assist your team in developing your why and creating a schedule that is responsive and equitable in which all students can thrive.

The journey to fully implementing the middle school concept can be met with challenges and questions. The concept has been evolving since the 1960s, so it stands to reason that your school may be a work in progress as well. This book, along with *The Successful Middle School: This We Believe* will help you prioritize your goals to develop the program that best meets the needs of the students in your school. The social, emotional, and academic needs of students ages 10–15 are different from their elementary and high school counterparts. Using your schedule to facilitate programming to address these needs will help your school make decisions that embrace the Essential Attributes of being responsive, challenging, empowering, equitable, and engaging.

CHAPTER 3: BELIEF STATEMENTS

The Successful Middle School: This We Believe
Characteristics Crossover

- Educators respect and value young adolescents
- Every student's academic and personal development is guided by an adult advocate

Part of developing our why is determining our **core beliefs**. Through the busyness of day-to-day activities, we can, at times, forget our reasons for becoming educators. At the time of this publication, every educator is experiencing a worldwide pandemic which has forced schools to close, caused overnight changes to learning platforms and the way we teach, and brought on continuous and daily uncertainty and challenges. What it hasn't done is change their core beliefs and what we know to be good for young adolescents. In fact, I believe it is these core beliefs that have made schools stronger and highlighted their dedication to students during this unprecedented time.

The Centre for Clinical Interventions defines core beliefs as "our very essence of how we see ourselves, other people, the world, and the future." Similarly, Sinek advises that core beliefs drive our behavior. I like to think that core beliefs are what ignite our passion as educators. As you begin your scheduling process, it is a good idea to establish the team's core beliefs and turn them into statements upon which your schedule will be built. **Those belief statements (sometimes called non-negotiables) will help drive the work of your scheduling team**.

You might be asking, what makes a belief statement different from the vision or mission statement? A belief statement, sometimes referred to as values, is directly tied to behavior. Merriam-Webster defines belief as "something that is accepted, considered to be true, or held as an opinion: something believed." When time is taken to clearly develop these beliefs, they serve as strong building blocks for the schedule as they are intimately tied to the culture. Belief statements tie the strategies directly to the why.

Team Exercise – Getting Started with Belief Statements

The 18 Characteristics are a wonderful place to start when developing your collective belief statements. Think about exercises that will familiarize your team and the entirety of middle school philosophy. One of the easiest exercises I have used is to display all 18 Characteristics and have your team rank them independently by color as follows:

- Green = We do this with consistency
- Yellow = We do this sometimes
- Red = Not yet (always use the growth mindset!)

This short activity helps you visualize how well your team feels they are implementing the 18 Characteristics as well as possible areas to prioritize with your scheduling. Areas that appear heavily in the green will indicate importance and that you are already doing them. Areas that appear heavily in yellow and red will need to be discussed as a team to determine their priority and how they translate in to what you develop in belief statements. Those statements can then be directly tied to the scheduling process.

For example, if "every student's academic and person development is guided by an adult advocate" is something that comes up in yellow or red, you may want to prioritize or discuss that as a belief statement. The belief statement may be that every child can learn and grow. This then translates into a structure for schedules as it has implications for counseling and/or advisory.

Characteristic	Green *We do this with consistency*	Yellow *We do this sometimes*	Red *Not yet*
Educators respect and value young adolescents.			
The school environment is welcoming, inclusive, and affirming for all.			
Every student's academic and personal development is guided by an adult advocate.			
School safety is addressed proactively, justly, and thoughtfully.			
Comprehensive counseling and support services meet the needs of young adolescents.			
The school engages families as valued partners.			
The school collaborates with community and business partners.			
Educators are specifically prepared to teach young adolescents and possess a depth of understanding in the content areas they teach.			
Curriculum is challenging, exploratory, integrative, and diverse.			

Health, wellness, and social-emotional competence are supported in curricula, school-wide programs, and related policies.			
Instruction fosters learning that is active, purposeful, and democratic.			
Varied and ongoing assessments advance learning as well as measure it.			
A shared vision developed by all stake-holders guides every decision.			
Policies and practices are student-centered, unbiased, and fairly implemented.			
Leaders are committed to and knowledgeable about young adolescents, equitable practices, and educational research.			
Leaders demonstrate courage and collaboration.			
Professional learning for all staff is relevant, long term, and job embedded.			
Organizational structures foster purposeful learning and meaningful relationships.			

Now that you have visualized areas of priority and growth and thoroughly discussed them, you are ready to get to belief statements. It is important to remember that belief is tied to behavior and to continually reflect on how these belief statements will tie to what the adults will be doing once the schedule is fully developed.

Below are some sample belief statements gathered from various groups with which I have worked. You will notice that these statements demonstrate a strong commitment to students and have clear ties to structures that you would consider including in your schedule.

Sample Belief Statements – from work completed in the field

- Every child can learn and grow
- Fair isn't everyone getting the same thing. Fair is everyone getting what they need to be successful
- School will feel safe, secure, and caring so that everyone has equal opportunity to succeed
- We value every child
- All students will succeed. Failure is not an option
- Learning is a collaborative process

For a more thorough exploration than this activity can provide, schools can also utilize The Successful Middle School Assessment. Using an anonymized survey instrument, the Assessment measures implementation of the 18 Characteristics through a series of evidence-based exemplars and teams can choose to also include versions designed for families and students. The assessment is coach-led and provides teams with a comprehensive report that baselines implementation and outlines areas of strength and growth. You can learn more at amle.org/SMS.

Expert Advice

- *Have fun developing belief statements. It is a time to bring out or even rekindling the passions of those on your team. View this as one of the most important things you will do in your scheduling process and not as a compliance activity. Belief statements should bring your group alive and fuel them!*
- *Continually refer to your belief statements and help the team evaluate the decisions that are being made and if they are honoring those belief statements. If one of your beliefs is that every child can learn and grow, but in the schedule not all students have access, it is a good indicator that the team must re-evaluate the structures in place for all students.*

CHAPTER 4: CULTURE

The Successful Middle School: This We Believe
Characteristics Crossover

- Policies and practices are student-centered, unbiased, and fairly implemented
- Leaders are committed to and knowledgeable about young adolescents, equitable practices, and educational research
- Leaders demonstrate courage and collaboration
- The school collaborates with community and business partners

"Culture trumps strategy every time."

– Harvard Business Review

I remember the first time I read that quote in the Harvard Business Review (2011). I had studied culture and strategy, but those five words together resonated with me. Any large-scale change we plan to do in our schools requires trust and a culture that is accepting of the change. There is power in the school schedule (a strategy), and it must be used wisely. To harness that power, school leaders must cultivate a positive and trusting school culture that is focused on learning and meeting the needs of students. Furthermore, they must ensure beliefs are aligned.

Let's first define the term culture. Merriam-Webster defines culture as "the set of shared attitudes, values, goals, and practices that characterizes an institution or organization." *The Successful Middle School: This We Believe* adds, "As architects for change, courageous, collaborative leaders make a difference by putting their knowledge and beliefs into action." Leaders have the enormous responsibility of answering this call to action by collaboratively developing their school schedule to meet the needs of all students. Reeves (2009) further asserts that culture is reflected in group or individual behavior, attitudes, and beliefs. He explains that leaders whose values seem contradictory can be one of the largest impediments to cultural change. Given this, leaders must continually reflect on their own beliefs and values to renew their sense of commitment to maintaining relationships, building trust, and most importantly, fostering a positive school culture.

Culture is perhaps most evident in the staff's attitudes toward their role. In his body of work, meta-analysis researcher John Hattie continually finds collective teacher efficacy as one of the highest effect sizes in schools today. Collective efficacy is the shared belief of the school/faculty staff in their ability to positively affect students. A school staff that believes it can accomplish great things and make a positive impact likely will (Bandura, 1997; Hattie, 2018). Meaningful collaboration on the schedule is one of the greatest demonstrations of collective efficacy a school leader can make.

Building our school culture to reflect a high level of efficacy and trust lays the groundwork for a schedule that is both based on student needs and widely accepted by staff as "what is best for the students." A change in the schedule is a big undertaking. Transparency throughout the process and building trust is vital. This is most easily accomplished by gathering the voices of your school community from the outset and involving as many stakeholders as possible. This will make your process relevant, accepted, benefited by collective wisdom, and inclusive of all voices.

Key stakeholders that teams may want to include are:

- all school staff;
- parents and caregivers;
- upper-level administration;
- students; and
- community advocates.

All of these groups can be included using surveys, focus groups, and committee work that pertains to developing the schedule. Committees could accomplish various objectives, including studying pedagogy best practices for instructing young adolescents, researching best practices for meeting the needs of the whole child to include social-emotional learning (SEL), collecting state mandates for minutes or course objectives, studying course offerings, and reviewing schedule examples from other school communities. Involving stakeholder voices in any of these ways will help the transparency of your process and expand the knowledge base for building a responsive schedule.

CHAPTER 5: START WITH A DIFFICULT CONVERSATION

"The courage to address tough topics comes from a deep commitment. No deep commitment, no hard dialogue."

– Anthony Muhammad

Beginning the process of creating a new schedule requires us to engage in conversations that can be difficult and that we may have been avoiding. The reality of a student-centered, responsive, and equitable schedule requires first answering this difficult question: "What *drives* your schedule?"

> **"What *drives* your schedule?"**

To help teams begin these conversations, I recommend engaging in the reflection exercise below and answering these questions: What is the current culture of your learning organization? If I were to look at your schedule from a 30,000-foot view, what would it say about your culture and beliefs?

Reflection Exercise

Review your current schedule. Make a list of the priorities or considerations that the schedule addresses and place them in the chart below. Remember to think about your "why" when completing this exercise.

Student Needs	Adult Needs	Initiatives or Mandates	State/ Federal Mandates
Example: Students need more opportunities for exploration	Example: Teachers prefer not to have multiple preps	Example: District has mandated time for Social-Emotional Learning	Example: Students must have a career exploration class by the completion of middle school

After completing this chart, reflect on the following questions:

- Are student needs the highest priority or consideration in your schedule?
- Is the learning of students and adults a high priority?
- What do the priorities say about your learning culture?

Expert Advice

- *Despite all the wonderful work you may do in building culture and creating impactful belief statements, there may still be naysayers. Lead with courage and know that meeting the needs of your students is the top priority and all decisions come from that place. Use the process to really prioritize the needs of your students and quiet the noise.*

CHAPTER 6: COLLECTIVE RESPONSIBILITY

The Successful Middle School: This We Believe
Characteristics Crossover

- Every student's academic and personal development is guided by an adult advocate
- Leaders demonstrate courage and collaboration

As earlier discussed in this book, the idea of collective efficacy and a school's ability to overcome obstacles and achieve their goals rests in their belief system. The beliefs are intimately linked to the culture and fostered through strong leadership and sound decision-making. When developing the schedule, a collaborative effort that involves stakeholders and listens to the voices of the community will be stronger and better reflect the needs of the school. Establishing a set of belief statements will help scheduling teams define their purpose and further establish the why of the schedule. The collective responsibility manifests itself in these belief statements and can help develop both the culture and technical paths of the schedule.

SECTION 1 REVIEW

Let's review the highlights of Section 1 to help you on your scheduling journey. If you have successfully completed the components suggested in Section 1 you will have:

1. Reviewed your vision and mission statements, ensuring they include action words that are specific to young adolescents.
2. Fully developed your why behind making a schedule change using belief statements that your team developed, guided by the 18 Characteristics of effective middle schools.
3. Reflected on the culture of your organization, prioritized needs, and addressed incongruencies through difficult conversations.
4. Fostered collective efficacy by involving stakeholders in your decision-making process.

I want to end Section 1 and begin Section 2 by pulling the two together. Recall that Figure 1.1 highlights both sides of scheduling (culture and strategy), and how they work together to create results. Our culture becomes our driving force, deeply rooted in the middle school philosophy and the 18 Characteristics. The schedule becomes the guiding path built on priorities, informed by data, and including the necessary building blocks for a responsive schedule.

SECTION 2

The How: Developing a Strategy for Creating a Responsive Middle School Schedule

- Tier 1 Instruction
- Data Review
- Root Cause Analysis
- The Voice of Equity in Scheduling
- The Voice of Students in Scheduling

The Scheduling Process

In Section 1 we explored the cultural aspects, or why, of creating school schedules. In this section, we will explore the how. This section will focus on determining your priorities by completing a full data review and needs assessment. Lastly, we will discuss the importance of equity and student voice in scheduling.

CHAPTER 1: TIER 1 INSTRUCTION

The Successful Middle School: This We Believe
Characteristics Crossover

- Educators are specifically prepared to teach young adolescents and possess a depth of understanding in the content areas they teach
- Curriculum is challenging, exploratory, integrative, and diverse
- Instruction fosters learning that is active, purposeful, and democratic

Before approaching a schedule change, it is important to review your Tier 1 instructional program. For the purpose of this book, Tier 1 is best described as quality instruction that teachers deliver, every day, designed to meet the needs of all students. For scheduling purposes, we must also understand the equation of targeted instruction + time = learning. (Buffum, Mattos, & Weber, 2012) When creating the schedule, allocation of Tier 1 instructional time is one of the most important considerations.

Through the data review process, teams should determine top priorities for Tier 1 instruction and student needs, ultimately leading them to decisions made for building blocks in the schedule. Time allocated to enrichment and intervention will also need to be determined, but this becomes part of the data review and building blocks discussion addressed later in this book. For more ideas on instruction for young adolescents, check out *The Successful Middle School: This We Believe*. Now let's get down with some data!

CHAPTER 2: DATA REVIEW

The Successful Middle School: This We Believe
Characteristics Crossover

- A shared vision developed by all stakeholders guides every decision
- Leaders demonstrate courage and collaborate
- Policies and practices are student-centered, unbiased, and fairly implemented

A critical component to completing a comprehensive and responsive schedule is a full review of all data sources. Given the responsibility that the schedule has to facilitate everyday operations of the school, this step is vital. A thorough review of all data sources will keep the team focused on the needs of students and set scheduling priorities. This phase helps the team begin to see actionable steps that embrace the previously developed belief statements.

"When schools create a collaborative culture around data use—when they use data not to point fingers but to inform collective decisions—something powerful can happen."

– Parker, 2007

> **A thorough review of all data sources will keep the team focused on the needs of students and set scheduling priorities.**

The Harvard Graduate School of Education developed the Data Wise Project to help educators engage in collaborative inquiry to focus on school improvement efforts. While the project focuses primarily on improving student achievement, the framework for data review helps to frame discussions for master scheduling. The Data Wise Improvement Process includes nine steps framed in the phases of Prepare, Inquire, and Act. Teams are encouraged to consider these phases in the process as they review their data:

- Prepare: Organizing for collaborative work
- Inquire: Creating a data overview, digging in, and examining
- Act: Developing the action plan

Prepare

As teams engage in the preparation phase of data, it is important to acknowledge that there are a variety of source types, all of which should be reviewed with a critical eye. Data sources to be collected can vary, but might include:

- academic achievement,
- student voice and/or satisfaction,
- staff and student surveys,
- focus group data, and
- discipline and attendance data.

Schools who engage in additional programming may also have data from external assessments or career exploration platforms.

Another source of data that teams may want to consider is the team-driven insights that can be harnessed using The Successful Middle School Assessment process. Conducted through a series of exemplars based on the 18 Characteristics, the data is solely driven by staff input, and parent and student input if desired, so it provides a comprehensive look at perspectives from and in all areas of the school. The team receives a detailed report with analysis and instruction on how to interpret the data contained in the report. Insights from this assessment can be used as a starting point for teams as they take a deeper look at all data sources from their building. Learn more at amle.org/sms

Inquire

To lead teams through the inquiry phase, consider evaluating the data through the lenses of cause and effect. Using these two lenses assists teams in determining relationships between presenting issues in the data and the true reasons behind them. Seeing data through these lenses can best be realized by engaging in data protocols, most specifically the root cause analysis. A root cause analysis is an approach to analyzing problems found in data before trying to solve them. Teams are encouraged to identify the problem and ask the question "why?" no less than five times, or use the familiar fishbone diagram. Resulting answers must be something that can be controlled by the organization, not outside forces.

Root Cause Analysis: How to Use the 5 Whys

- Write down the problem and be specific about exactly what it is.
- Begin asking why the problem exists, only including answers that are in your control.
- Once you have asked "why?" five times, you should be at the root cause. If not, keep asking until you have agreement. Remember that the root cause has to be something that you can control.

Root Cause Analysis: How to Use the Fishbone Diagram

- Write the problem statement in the head of the fish.
- It may be helpful to label larger areas on the fish as you begin to think of causes. Some examples could be curriculum, culture, materials, space, staff, time.
- In the skeleton of the fish consider possible causes and list them, consider data sources you have to back up the statements.
- As you are listing causes, ask "why?"
- *It may be helpful to label them as related to adults or students, and then cross off the ones that are labeled with students.*

Fishbone Diagram

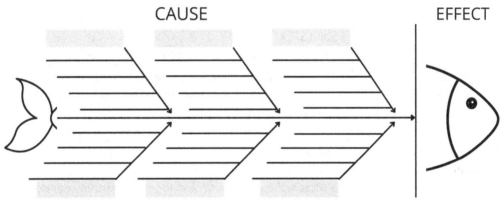

To help with the data inquiry process, I have created questions for teams to consider based on areas that are directly related to scheduling. Questions are organized by themes, which will help teams in prioritizing data and action planning for the schedule. This part of the inquiry phase is one of the most important parts to truly building a responsive schedule as teams may discover gaps or issues that were not previously considered. It is recommended that teams who find gaps or issues after answering these questions perform the root cause analysis to really get to the issue and then create the plan during the action phase.

School Demographics	<ul><li>How many students are enrolled in the school?</li><li>How many students are part of special populations?</li><li>How many certified and non-certified staff are in the building?</li></ul>
Academic Achievement	<ul><li>Does core instruction meet the needs of at least 80% of students?</li><li>Do you have achievement gaps?</li><li>What are the student achievement rates on various measures?</li></ul>
Intervention and Enrichment	<ul><li>Do students need increased instructional time?</li><li>Is there time in the day specifically for intervention and/or enrichment that does not detract from other courses?</li><li>What provisions need to be made at school for students who have outside needs?</li></ul>
Discipline, Attendance, and Social-Emotional Learning	<ul><li>Number of discipline referrals, reasons, and consequences.</li><li>What is the current attendance rate for all students? Student subgroups?</li><li>Do you need time in the day to address mental health and SEL?</li><li>What is the current student satisfaction rate?</li></ul>
Teaming and Course Pathways	<ul><li>Do you have the structures in place to support teaming?</li><li>Does your school offer high school credits and is there a pathway for students?</li><li>Is teaming impacted by these courses?</li></ul>
Advanced Courses and Equity	<ul><li>Do all students have access to advanced courses?</li><li>Are there opportunity gaps?</li><li>What is the enrollment data in your advanced courses?</li><li>Do students have a voice in choosing their schedules, most specifically, when it comes to advanced courses?</li><li>Are there strict guidelines that prevent all students from accessing advanced courses?</li></ul>
Themes and Trends	<ul><li>As you were reflecting on your data, what themes or trends did you discuss?</li><li>Are any of them created by the current schedule?</li><li>How might you begin to address them through the schedule?</li></ul>

Act

Equipped with the insights you've gained through preparation and inquiry; you will be ready to act to create a responsive school schedule. We will dig into action in Section 3, but first let's be sure to see our data through the lenses of equity and student voice before proceeding.

CHAPTER 3: THE VOICE OF EQUITY IN SCHEDULING

The Successful Middle School: This We Believe
Characteristics Crossover

- Every student's academic and personal development is guided by an adult advocate
- Leaders demonstrate courage and collaborate
- Policies and practices are student-centered, unbiased, and fairly implemented

In the last section of this exercise, your team began to tackle one of the largest disparities in P–12 education: access to advanced courses. Middle school is a time of exploration, but it is also a time where students are typically engaging in their first experiences with advanced- or high school credit–bearing classes. Historically, this has been seen as a middle school issue; however, it can be rooted in practices that start in elementary school. In January 2020, the Education Trust released its most current report, which included the following data points as it relates to unequal representation of Black and Latino/a students in Advanced Coursework.

- **Elementary school**: Black students represent 16% of overall enrollment in elementary schools, but only 9% of enrollment in gifted and talented programs; Latino/a students are 28% of students enrolled in elementary schools, but only 18% of those in gifted and talented programs.
- **Middle school**: Black and Latino/a students are not adequately enrolled in eighth grade algebra. Black students make up 15% of eighth graders, but only 10% of students enrolled in eighth grade Algebra I. Similarly, Latino students make up 25% of eighth graders and just 18% of eighth graders in the course.

- **High school**: Black and Latino students are locked out of Advanced Placement (AP). Black students make up 15% of high schoolers nationwide, but only 9% of students enrolled in at least one AP course. Nearly a quarter of students are Latino, but only 21% of students enrolled in AP courses are Latino.[1]

Similar data can be found for either twice-exceptional or special education students. Needs that are addressed through individualized education plans can prevent students from accessing advanced courses when not carefully scheduled. Access to advanced coursework in high school typically begins in middle school with the offerings of high school credit classes. Some even start in elementary! Students who are not scheduled with both their strengths and their needs in mind find themselves tracked in a pathway that limits their access. One study by Susan Shultz (2012) showed that early placement decisions of twice-exceptional students negatively impacted their enrollment in AP courses.

> **When not carefully examined, schedules can create opportunity gaps.**

These data points are included in this section because opportunity gaps can often be addressed through the schedule but are far too often overlooked. In *The Glossary of Education Reform*, an opportunity gap is defined as "ways in which race, ethnicity, socioeconomic status, English proficiency, community wealth, familial situations, or other factors contribute to or perpetuate lower educational aspirations, achievement, and attainment for certain groups of students." When not carefully examined, schedules can create opportunity gaps. As teams begin the scheduling process, they can review their collected data and ensure that clear pathways are available to all students and opportunity gaps are avoided. While these discussions are sometimes difficult, they are a necessary step in truly creating an equitable and responsive schedule.

---

1 *The Civil Rights Data Collection no longer reports the number of students taking world languages. However, data from College Board suggest that the overall representation of Latino students in AP is slightly inflated by participation in AP Spanish. In 2018, Latino students took 23% of all advanced placement exams and 71% of the AP Spanish and Culture exams

Expert Advice

- Advanced or high school courses can at times be in conflict with teaming. Carefully examine your scheduling practices and think creatively about how you team or cohort your students to ensure that your classes and teams are equitably created. It might require outside of the box thinking and some unconventional teaming configurations, but in the end, it is part of creatively scheduling to meet the needs of all students and avoid opportunity gaps.
- Some solutions are cross-teaming for certain classes, switching teachers for different periods to teach students from another team, and avoiding cohorting of advanced courses. This practice can create an entire cohort of singletons in your schedule which can appear to look like tracking.
- Course recommendations and prerequisites: Carefully examine your practices and look for adult-created policies that affect student access to courses. I prefer to have as few as possible.
- Ensure proper supports for all students who engage in advanced courses, most specifically those who may be overlooked because of artificial requirements , labels, or language proficiency status.

CHAPTER 4: THE VOICE OF STUDENTS IN SCHEDULING

Through the process of creating the schedule, teams should make sure that student voice does not get lost. In Section 1 we discuss surveying students or creating student focus groups to get input on the schedule. In the data dive in Section 2, we look specifically at student data and the needs of the students. But as we create courses and offerings, this is where we must also consider the student voice. Middle school is a time of exploration and sorting through things. Schedules can help facilitate or thwart that process. Teams will need to consider which elective choices or high school courses are available to students to choose. Additionally, there is the decision of whether students choose their electives or if exploration will be through the creation of a "wheel" class for electives. A wheel class is a variety of classes offered for a given period of time (e.g., 9 weeks, trimester, or shorter intervals) that students take as an exploratory class. Teams may decide this is a good option for their youngest students or all students. Regardless of what is decided, student voice should be important in guiding these decisions.

SECTION 2 REVIEW

Let's review the highlights of Section 2 to help you on your scheduling journey. If you have successfully completed the components suggested in Section 2 you will have:

- Completed a full review of all data types to inform your scheduling process.
- Conducted root cause analysis(s) for issues or trends identified in your data that can be addressed through the schedule. For example, maybe courses are blocking each other, or unnecessary requirements are keeping students out of advanced courses.
- Considered both the voice of equity and students in your scheduling process. When answering all the questions in the grid you may discover that your schedule has unintentionally created opportunity gaps or kept students out of courses, and this is your chance to fix that.

I want to end Section 2 and begin Section 3 by pulling the two together. Figure 1.1 highlights both sides of scheduling (culture and strategy), and how they work together to create results. Our culture becomes our driving path, deeply rooted in the middle school philosophy and grounded in the 18 Characteristics. The schedule becomes the guiding path built on priorities, decided by data, and including the necessary building blocks for a responsive schedule. Section 3 becomes the action phase where you will dig into components of your schedule and really get to work!

SECTION 3

The What: Creating a Responsive Middle School Schedule

- The Scheduling Team
- Primary Building Blocks
- Key Elements of Middle School Schedules
- Types of Schedules
- Traditional Schedule Options
- Block Schedule Options
- Top 10 Rules for Scheduling

The Scheduling Process

In Section 2 we began exploring the technical aspects of school scheduling, initiating the preparing and inquiry phases of data review. Now that you and your team have reflected on your beliefs, climate, and culture, and have officially completed the deep dive into data, it's time for action. It is not enough just to study the 18 Characteristics; it is our imperative to put them into action. Section 3 will focus on specific action steps and considerations that teams should take as they progress through their work. In this section, we will explore how your school can develop the team to work through the building blocks of the schedule and their roles and responsibilities. Additionally, you will find a variety of schedule types that include both the benefits and challenges to help in your decision-making process. This section is concluded with my recommended rules for scheduling that have proven to be effective over the years.

CHAPTER 1: THE SCHEDULING TEAM

The Successful Middle School: This We Believe
Characteristics Crossover

- A shared vision developed by all stakeholders guides every decision
- Every student's academic and personal development is guided by an adult advocate
- Organizational structure fosters purposeful learning and meaningful relationships

As part of the collaborative process for creating the schedule, schools should also develop the scheduling team. The scheduling team is tasked with developing the master schedule considering all of the work that has been done prior to starting. This team's job is to turn the synthesized data and feedback into a working master schedule. They will work on creating schedule options and communicating and gathering feedback to inform the process.

Using the team structure helps for a collective approach that plays into the strengths and knowledge of those representatives. Varying the experience, knowledge, and talents of the scheduling team creates an inclusive process with multiple perspectives. Some teams may elect to create roles in their team and norms for this group should also be considered. This team will be a subset of your larger staff representing administration, student services, multiple grade levels, and a variety of contents. Scheduling teams often include specialists, assessments specialists, and sometimes parents/community members.

Deciding who will make up the scheduling team is an important decision; it will be up to each organization to determine what is the best makeup for them. I suggest thinking about including the following roles or voices to be on your team. Below are their names and the role they will play in the process. Roles can be added, but I don't recommend eliminating any of these.

Use the following "characters" who will help write the "story" of your schedule:

- **The Student**. The schedule is always about the students. Keep a team member on board to be the student voice to ensure that it doesn't get lost in competing interests.
- **The Visionary**. The visionary is charged with always remembering the vision, mission, goals, and beliefs. They should be a big picture person. ~~who dreams big!~~
- **The Worker**. This is the person who will "do the work." They may spend time researching, creating new versions, and completing tasks. They help to keep the group on task and moving forward. They pair nicely with the thinker!
- **The Thinker**. The thinker may be both creative and analytical. They will easily see the puzzle that makes the schedule and have creative ways to work around problems. They tend to have a mathematical brain but can be governed by the right brain. They are sometimes referred to as the schedule guru.
- **The Creative Extrovert**. This is the counterpart to the thinker. They see things differently. This is the person on your team who will continue to come up with ideas to solve problems, no matter how outrageous they might be. They may at times clash with the group, but their ideas can be shaped into solutions.
- **The Healer**. The healer plays the important role of remembering that schedules must encompass the social, academic, and personal needs of students. They see the schedule through the eyes of other providers and the essential role they play in the development of the young adolescent. They may also be helpful if the extrovert and the naysayer clash.
- **The Naysayer**. We all know one, but we don't always think they need to be on the team. Wrong. It is important to have all the voices, even those

who may be cynical or doubtful. This voice becomes important because they will see and express potential pitfalls. They might clash with the creative extrovert, but they will represent those who struggle with change.

- **The Enforcer**. This is your team member who always follows the rules. They will help keep your team focused and moving toward achieving your goals of the responsive schedule. They pair nicely with the visionary. This should be a person who is effective at navigating difficult conversations and has a good rapport with everyone else on the team.

Team Refinement Exercise

Decide the roles or voices that you want people to play on your team and the primary responsibilities they will be facilitating. Create a chart that reflects these roles and responsibilities. Have each member of your scheduling team place their name and their individual strengths on sticky notes—one strength per sticky. When finished, have each team member place their stickies on the chart where they feel their strengths most apply. This will help you refine and assign the roles!

Sample Chart

Scheduling Team Role	Primary Responsibilities	Strengths by Individual
Example: *Ann–The Thinker*	*Example:* *Identifies roadblocks that might be created by the schedule* *Helps the team brainstorm ways around conflicts*	*Example:* *Strategic thinker* *Good at figuring out puzzles/ problems*

CHAPTER 2: PRIMARY BUILDING BLOCKS

The Successful Middle School: This We Believe
Characteristics Crossover

- Educators are specifically prepared to teach young adolescents and possess a depth of understanding in the content areas they teach
- Health, wellness, and social-emotional competence are supported in curricula, school-wide programs, and related policies
- Organizational structure fosters purposeful learning and meaningful relationships
- Leaders demonstrate courage and collaboration

This section will help teams consider what is needed to make scheduling decisions. While many schedules will seem perfect on paper, it is not until you think through these building blocks that will signal whether something will work or not. Completing this part of the process helps the team understand their limitations or outlines items they may need to advocate for in creating their ideal schedule.

Expert Advice

- This step is first in this book on purpose. Make sure you don't skip this step—it is what I call the reality check of scheduling. This will let you know where you are starting and how far you may have to go to achieve your dream schedule.

Fleshing out this information will translate directly to building the schedule. Let's get started!

Time. Next to our students, time is the most precious resource. As you begin the scheduling process, think about time in terms of minutes per day and where it will be spent. Establish your start time, how long your periods will be, time spent in transitions, and lunch. If your data leads to decisions of extra time needed in different areas, it must be discussed at this time. I recommend starting with your total minutes, subtracting lunch and minimum pass times (these are non-negotiable).

Classes. The team will need to establish how many classes will be offered in a day. Special programming may require additional periods and will need to be considered. Teams who want to offer either intervention or enrichment will need to decide if these will be specific classes or a separate period created to address these needs. During this part, the team will also need to decide if there will be elective or exploratory classes, and how many. Middle school is designed to be a time of exploration with increasing student choice; the team will have to balance these as they make these decisions.

> **Middle school is designed to be a time of exploration with increasing student choice**

Staffing. This consideration boils down to how much you have. If you are considering extended time, teaming, or special programming, think about how much more you will need. It is good to start with your current number and know what the limitations of the schedule could be should you be faced with making changes without additional staff.

Teacher Assignments. Teaching assignments are complex. It is not only a game of certification and negotiated contracts, but also near and dear to everyone's heart. Deciding who teaches what and how many is one of the most difficult things that administrators deal with when creating the schedule. Teaching assignments are part of equity for staff and students. The team should consider teaching loads and preps. It is possible that this is something that is already in policy—make sure you check! Alongside that process, teams should ensure that specific students are matched with the most qualified teachers. A good data dive will help teams match teacher strengths with student needs.

Special Populations. It is important to know your numbers and services offered. During the process, the team should consider a continuum of options for students that is responsive to their needs and aligned with inclusive practices. The opportunity gap section of the data review may have uncovered issues that need to be addressed and this is a good opportunity to think through addressing them.

Lunch and/or Recess. How much time will it be? While we know that lunch is a mandatory activity, recess is not. Recess is a much-debated topic that the team will need to research and decide. It is not in this section for debate, but for teams to realize that if decided to be a part of the schedule, time will need to be allocated.

Other Mandatory Time Takers. These can come in a variety of sizes and shapes but are often forgotten when creating the schedule. Think through initiatives at the school or district level that may require time in the day and plan for them.

CHAPTER 3: KEY ELEMENTS OF MIDDLE SCHOOL SCHEDULES

The Successful Middle School: This We Believe
Characteristics Crossover

- Every student's academic and personal development is guided by an adult advocate
- Comprehensive counseling and support services meet the needs of young adolescents
- Health, wellness, and social-emotional competence are supported in curricula, school-wide programs, and related policies
- Curriculum is challenging, exploratory, integrative, and diverse
- Professional learning for all staff is relevant, long-term, and job-embedded
- Organizational structure fosters purposeful learning and meaningful relationships

The 18 Characteristics provide us with suggestions for key elements of middle school schedules. In addition to the research and practice in *The Successful Middle School*, Hattie's research adds additional data that helps in the decision-making process. The 18 Characteristics help us to know what makes the middle school concept and Hattie's research backs up high effect sizes, ultimately giving insight into scheduling strategies. Hattie's work has shown the impact of the following effect sizes which we can then translate directly into elements of the schedule.

Effect Size	Mean Effect Size	Tied To
Teacher Collective Efficacy (2017)	1.57	Teaming and professional learning communities
Response to Intervention (2017)	1.29	Intervention and enrichment periods
Teacher Relationships (2015)	.72	Advisory

When starting a middle school schedule, leaders and teams are faced with making the decision of how to organize both teachers and students. The middle school concept recommends using the teaming structure to complete this process. "A signature component of middle schooling is the interdisciplinary team of two or more teachers working with a common group of students for a shared block of time, ideally in a proximate space" (AMLE, 2020). In addition to teaming, schools are encouraged to schedule time for professional learning communities (PLC). These two powerful structures built into a schedule provide the framework for teachers to focus on students and academics.

Teaming. *The Successful Middle School: This We Believe* notes that teams provide the foundation for a strong learning community and can positively influence a "student's sense of belonging, social bonding, and connectedness." Creating teacher teams consists of combining staff to share students in common. These teams are interdisciplinary in nature and help create the family feel in middle school. These teachers will work together to create an experience for students that is connected academically, socially, and personally. These smaller structures within the school help students make the developmental leap from elementary to middle school.

The Successful Middle School: This We Believe further notes that the teaming structure "also offers positive outcomes for teachers' professional lives, with the potential to expand collegiality, bolster support, and enhance professional growth" (AMLE, 2020). In addition to multiple position papers, the National Staff Development Council noted that professional development at the middle school level be results driven, standards-based, and embedded in the daily working for teachers (McCarty, 2010). This professional experience can best be realized through the implementation of professional learning communities. Schedulers can achieve this type of job-embedded professional development by scheduling teams and teachers with time to meet and plan during the day.

Expert Advice

- *Teaming configurations can be different at every school. Teams consist of more than 2 teachers who share students in common. They frequently also include Intervention Specialists or those to teach English Language Development. Interdisciplinary teams will include those from the elective areas. The set-up of teams will vary on size and make-up of the school. Schedulers should consider the expertise, experience, and certification of the teachers when creating teams as well as the desired size of the team.*
- *Something that I like to do in my scheduling is ask teachers what types of teams they would create and why? I also like to create a number of different options for them and get their input. Providing teachers with a voice in the process is important. Synergistic teams are good for students and fostering that from the beginning is a vital step.*
- *For additional ideas on Teaming be sure to check out the AMLE resources and book store.*

Professional Learning Communities or Collaborative Teams. To meet the academic, social, and personal needs of young adolescents, teams should have common planning time which helps to facilitate professional learning communities or collaborative teams. In the same way that teaming shares students, professional learning communities share content. Combining these two organizational structures allows schools to make the most of their schedule and meet the needs of students. A core belief of professional learning communities is that all students can succeed at high levels (Dufour,2011). To achieve this goal and ensure high levels of learning, collaborative teams engage in rich discussion centered around instruction, assessment, enrichment, and intervention. By continually setting goals and reflecting on their practice, middle school collaborative teams can give life to all the Characteristics included within Curriculum, Instruction, and Assessment. Through the teaming and PLC process, teams can effectively discuss student needs and plan for intervention, enrichment, and social-emotional needs.

Response to Intervention. High-functioning teams and professional learning communities are a first line of defense in planning and providing responsive instruction for students. However, sometimes students need more. As stated in the section on Tier 1 instruction, we must understand the equation of targeted instruction + time = learning. In *Simplifying Response to Intervention*, Buffum, Mattos, and Weber (2012) guide teams through the process of providing students additional time to create circumstances for high levels of learning for each student. If through the data dive process, teams recognize that more time is needed in specific content areas, then time needs to be allocated. This time can be realized through the creation of intervention and enrichment courses or a specific period in the day.

Advisory. In my opinion, one of the most beautiful times in a middle school day is Advisory! This is the time set apart where we focus holistically on the child, make meaningful connections, and place a priority on relationships. Advisory is a way for schools to truly advocate for their students and involve all the adults in the school. According to *The Successful Middle School: This We Believe*, "The purpose of this time is to provide academic and social-emotional mentorship and support, to create a sense of belonging and community within the school, and to facilitate a small community of learners." Discussions and information gleaned during Advisory time can also help schools put students in touch with resources both in and out of the school. It is not a secret that young adolescents are regularly navigating unsteady waters; but through the guidance of a trusted adult, they can grow and strengthen their oars. If your belief statements include advocacy and growing students, including time in your schedule for this to happen includes planning for Advisory.

CHAPTER 4: TYPES OF SCHEDULES

As you begin to read and brainstorm this section, remember that for every schedule you see, there could be hundreds of variations. I often say that scheduling is an art and that schedulers should be creative. This is where it starts. I also want to provide you with these four guiding questions that you could write down and answer as you create:

- How much is this going to cost?
- Is this in line with our governing documents, whether contract or policy?
- How much change will need to take place to make this happen?
- What professional development will be needed to ensure that staff is properly prepared?

In school scheduling there are two prominent types of schedules: traditional and block. In a traditional schedule, students attend all their classes every day for a specific amount of time (45–50 minutes). In a block period, the instructional periods are longer (90–110) minutes and students attend them every other day. Both types of schedules have benefits and challenges. It will be up to the team to decide which best meets their needs. This section will provide you with samples of traditional and block schedules. Given the importance of Advisory to the middle school concept, you will see that time is allotted in these samples. These schedules will represent the average length of a typical middle school day based on information from the National Center of Educational Statistics.

CHAPTER 5: TRADITIONAL SCHEDULE OPTIONS

8 Period Traditional

The 8 Period Traditional schedule consists of 8 same-length classes that meet every day. Depending on the length of the day, these periods usually run from 42–45 minutes. During an 8 Period Day, students will typically transition 7 or 8 times depending on how the lunch is structured and up to 9 if Advisory is a stand-alone period.

Figure 1.2- 8 Period Traditional

Class	Begin	End	Length
Advisory	8:00 AM	8:26 AM	26
Pass	8:26 AM	8:29 AM	3
1	8:29 AM	9:12 AM	43
Pass	9:12 AM	9:15 AM	3
2	9:15 AM	9:58 AM	43
Pass	9:58 AM	10:01 AM	3
3	10:01 AM	10:44 AM	43
Pass	10:44 AM	10:46 AM	2
Lunch	10:46 AM	11:16 AM	30
Pass	11:16 AM	11:18 AM	2
4	11:18 AM	12:01 PM	43
Pass	12:01 PM	12:04 PM	3
5	12:04 PM	12:47 PM	43
Pass	12:47 PM	12:50 PM	3
6	12:50 PM	1:33 PM	43
Pass	1:33 PM	1:36 PM	3
7	1:36 PM	2:19 PM	43
Pass	2:19 PM	2:22 PM	3
8	2:22 PM	3:05 PM	43

Benefits

- Teachers see students every day
- An 8 Period Day provides more flexibility in the schedule, allowing for additional sections to be created
- Students can have more options in the schedule
- With the additional periods, it is easy to add intervention, enrichment, or double-period courses
- Good for classes that may need daily reinforcement
- Familiar

Challenges

- Does not allow for extended learning opportunities
- Length of instructional periods may limit pedagogy
- Time lost during transitions
- Fragmented day for students

7 Period Traditional

The 7 Period Traditional schedule consists of 7 same-length classes that meet every day. Depending on the length of the day, these periods usually run from 47–52 minutes. During a 7 Period Day, students will typically transition 6 or 7 times depending on how the lunch is structured and up to 8 if Advisory is a stand-alone period.

Figure 1.3- 7 Period Traditional

Class	Begin	End	Length
Advisory	8:00 AM	8:28 AM	28
Pass	8:28 AM	8:31 AM	3
1	8:31 AM	9:20 AM	49
Pass	9:20 AM	9:23 AM	3
2	9:23 AM	10:12 AM	49
Pass	10:12 AM	10:15 AM	3
3	10:15 AM	11:04 AM	49
Pass	11:04 AM	11:07 AM	3
Lunch	11:07 AM	11:37 AM	30
Pass	11:37 AM	11:40 AM	3
4	11:40 AM	12:29 PM	49
Pass	12:29 PM	12:32 PM	3
5	12:32 PM	1:21 PM	49
Pass	1:21 PM	1:24 PM	3
6	1:24 PM	2:13 PM	49
Pass	2:13 PM	2:16 PM	3
7	2:16 PM	3:05 PM	49

Benefits

- Teachers see students every day
- Good for classes that may need daily reinforcement
- With the additional time, intervention and/or enrichment could be added to the day
- Familiar

Challenges

- Does not allow for extended learning opportunities
- Length of instructional periods may limit pedagogy
- Time lost during transitions
- Fragmented day for students

6 Period Traditional

The 6 Period Traditional schedule consists of 6 same-length classes that meet every day. Depending on the length of the day, these periods usually run from 55–60 minutes. During a 6 Period Day, students will typically transition 4 or 5 times depending on how the lunch is structured and up to 7 if Advisory is a stand-alone period.

Figure 1.4- 6 Period Traditional

Class	Begin	End	Length
Advisory	8:00 AM	8:26 AM	26
Pass	8:26 AM	8:29 AM	3
1	8:29 AM	9:27 AM	58
Pass	9:27 AM	9:30 AM	3
2	9:30 AM	10:28 AM	58
Pass	10:28 AM	10:31 AM	3
3	10:31 AM	11:29 AM	58
Pass	11:29 AM	11:32 AM	3
Lunch	11:32 AM	12:02 PM	30
Pass	12:02 PM	12:05 PM	3
4	12:05 PM	1:03 PM	58
Pass	1:03 PM	1:06 PM	3
5	1:06 PM	2:04 PM	58
Pass	2:04 PM	2:07 PM	3
6	2:07 PM	3:05 PM	58

Benefits

- Teachers see students every day
- Instructional periods are longer
- Good for classes that may need daily reinforcement
- Limits the courses that can be offered
- With the additional time, intervention and/or enrichment could be added to the day
- Familiar

Challenges

- Length of instructional periods can be difficult for teachers to plan because they are neither traditional nor block
- Time lost during transitions
- Fragmented day for students

CHAPTER 6: BLOCK SCHEDULE OPTIONS

Block schedules emerged in the 1990s (Brasel & Gill, 1999), with close to 40% of high schools having full block schedules by 2002 (Rettig, 2002). High schools chose block schedules to provide students and teachers with longer instructional periods, to decrease time spent in transitions thus lowering hallway issues and discipline, and were said to calm the environment in the school (Rettig, 2000). The original *This We Believe* highlighted the learning needs of young adolescents, most specifically the pedagogy. They recommended active learning, multiple teaching approaches, and exploratory curriculum—all of which can be facilitated during the longer instructional periods of time.

8 Period Block

The 8 Period Block, also sometimes known as the 4X4, consists of 8 longer periods that meet every other day and range from 90–100 minutes. For middle school, these classes typically meet every other day for the full year. In a true 4X4 schedule, the student will attend 4 block classes every day for a semester. In a typical day of block, there may be 4 or 5 transitions. Not shown on the model below, but one block typically includes lunch which is either before, during, or after the period.

Figure 1.5- 8 Period Block Sample

Class	Begin	End	Length
Advisory	8:00 AM	8:24 AM	24
Pass	8:24 AM	8:27 AM	3
1/2	8:27 AM	9:56 AM	89
Pass	9:56 AM	9:59 AM	3
3/4	9:59 AM	11:28 AM	89
Pass	11:28 AM	11:31 AM	3
Lunch	11:31 AM	12:01 PM	30
Pass	12:01 PM	12:04 PM	3
5/6	12:04 PM	1:33 PM	89
Pass	1:33 PM	1:36 PM	3
7/8	1:36 PM	3:05 PM	89

Benefits

- Increased instructional time
- Fewer transitions
- Calmer environment with less discipline
- Ability to complete cross-curricular projects
- 8 period allows for flexibility by creating more courses offered
- Period 8 can be used as a flex period to provide intervention, enrichment, or to create more time in other subjects
- High level of engagement with proper planning

Challenges

- Pedagogy can be challenging when not properly planned
- Requires appropriate professional development
- Poor planning and execution, and can be difficult for some populations

7 Period Block

The 7 Period Block consists of 6 longer periods that meet every other day and range from 95–110 minutes, and one singleton that meets every day for 50–55 minutes. The addition of the singleton period allows teams to anchor Advisory or create an additional intervention or enrichment period attached to that same period. The singleton can be a great class to strategically schedule courses that may need an everyday attendance. In a typical day, there may be 4 or 5 transitions. Not shown on the model below, but one block typically includes lunch which is either before, during, or after the period.

Figure 1.6- 7 Period Block Sample

Class	Begin	End	Length
Advisory	8:00 AM	8:25 AM	25
Pass	8:25 AM	8:28 AM	3
1/2	8:28 AM	10:08 AM	100
Pass	10:08 AM	10:11 AM	3
3	10:11 AM	11:06 AM	55
Pass	11:06 AM	11:09 AM	3
4/5	11:09 AM	12:49 PM	100
Pass	12:49 PM	12:52 PM	3
Lunch	12:52 PM	1:22 PM	30
Pass	1:22 PM	1:25 PM	3
6/7	1:25 PM	3:05 PM	100

Benefits

- Increased instructional time
- Fewer transitions
- Calmer environment with less discipline
- Ability to complete cross-curricular projects
- High level of engagement with proper planning
- Singleton can be used to creatively schedule specific classes

Challenges

- Pedagogy can be challenging when not properly planned
- Requires appropriate professional development
- Poor planning and execution, and can be
- difficult for some populations
- Some teachers may have difficulty navigating the difference in pacing for block vs. singleton period

6 Period Block

The 6 Period Block consists of 6 same-length classes of 110–120 minutes that meet every other day for an entire year. Upon first review, the 6 Period Block looks a bit more limiting than other schedules; however, schools can use these large chunks of time to complete more flexible time activities and/or create additional classes by splitting classes. Seen a different way, the 6 Period Block schedule can also create very long periods of learning for students and is sometimes adopted by schools who are looking to improve academics in specific areas or limit courses offered to students. In a 6 Period Block, there are usually 3–4 transitions when scheduled as the model below. Depending on what all a school does with this model, students may spend more time in transition.

Figure 1.7- 6 Period Block Sample

Class	Begin	End	Length
Advisory	8:00 AM	8:25 AM	25
Pass	8:25 AM	8:30 AM	5
1/2	8:30 AM	10:28 AM	118
Pass	10:28 AM	10:33 AM	5
3/4	10:33 AM	12:31 PM	118
Lunch	12:31 PM	1:01 PM	30
3	1:01 PM	1:06 PM	5
5/6	1:06 PM	3:05 PM	119

Benefits

- Increased instructional time
- Fewer transitions
- Calmer environment with less discipline
- Ability to complete cross-curricular projects
- High level of engagement with proper planning
- Classes can be split to create more options for students during the day
- Time can be used flexibly by teams to meet team and individual students needs

42

Challenges

- Pedagogy can be challenging when not properly planned
- Requires appropriate professional development
- Poor planning and execution, and can be
- difficult for some populations
- If used only for 6 periods, limits the courses available to students

Flexible Time in Block Schedules

Regardless of the type of block schedule you choose, time can and should be considered flexible and used by teams of teachers to meet the needs of students. Rettig (2002) noted that middle school schedules should be flexible, allowing teachers to use a variety of teaching strategies and integrated curriculum. To further this point, *The Successful Middle School: This We Believe* recommends integrated curriculum through "thoughtfully designed interdisciplinary experiences, studies, and units that help students see the integrated nature of knowledge and the many connections that link various topics, concepts, and subjects" (p.30). To create these types of curricular experiences that include inquiry and action, longer periods of instructional time will be needed for teachers. Flexibility in how that time is spent can help facilitate these opportunities. Lastly, a flexible schedule allows teachers to pace the curriculum as needed and not rush through an activity because of a bell.

Hybrid/Alternative Day Schedules

One in three schools today still have a block schedule (Retting for AASA). Due to the many identified challenges of block schedules, schools abandoned the practice and returned to either a traditional schedule, or what I like to call the "somewhere in the middle" schedule, known as the Hybrid or Alternative Day schedules. It is important to note that in this book, hybrid refers to two types of schedules, not who is in attendance, a term that emerged during the pandemic to accommodate social distancing requirements. In a hybrid schedule, school teams choose any of the traditional and block schedules and combine them either by alternating days or creating some type of rotation with the days. This schedule type allows for at least one to two block periods a week to accommodate teachers who want to take advantage of those longer periods of instruction, but compromise with the traditional periods where they will see students every period. The example below shows how a school might run the traditional schedule on Monday and then follow Tuesday–Friday on the block. Some schools may choose more traditional than block days and some vice versa. Regardless of what they choose, they get to experience both sides of scheduling.

Figure Figure 1.8- Hybrid/Alternative Schedule

Class	Begin	End	Length
Advisory	8:00 AM	8:26 AM	26
Pass	8:26 AM	8:29 AM	3
1	8:29 AM	9:12 AM	43
Pass	9:12 AM	9:15 AM	3
2	9:15 AM	9:58 AM	43
Pass	9:58 AM	10:01 AM	3
3	10:01 AM	10:44 AM	43
Pass	10:44 AM	10:46 AM	2
Lunch	10:46 AM	11:16 AM	30
Pass	11:16 AM	11:18 AM	2
4	11:18 AM	12:01 PM	43
Pass	12:01 PM	12:04 PM	3
5	12:04 PM	12:47 PM	43
Pass	12:47 PM	12:50 PM	3
6	12:50 PM	1:33 PM	43
Pass	1:33 PM	1:36 PM	3
7	1:36 PM	2:19 PM	43
Pass	2:19 PM	2:22 PM	3
8	2:22 PM	3:05 PM	43

Class	Begin	End	Length
Advisory	8:00 AM	8:24 AM	24
Pass	8:24 AM	8:27 AM	3
1/2	8:27 AM	9:56 AM	89
Pass	9:56 AM	9:59 AM	3
3/4	9:59 AM	11:28 AM	89
Pass	11:28 AM	11:31 AM	3
Lunch	11:31 AM	12:01 PM	30
Pass	12:01 PM	12:04 PM	3
5/6	12:04 PM	1:33 PM	89
Pass	1:33 PM	1:36 PM	3
7/8	1:36 PM	3:05 PM	89

Traditional Day (Monday)   **Block Days (Tuesday-Friday)**

Benefits

- Schools get exposure to both longer and shorter instructional periods
- Time saved on transitions from block days could be used to add an intervention or enrichment period
- On traditional days, teachers see all students
- In short weeks, schools can use either the traditional or block schedule to keep days balanced

Challenges

- Pedagogy on block days will need to be different and teachers will need proper professional development
- Pacing between traditional and block days can be challenging for teachers
- If schools choose only two block days and students miss school, it can be difficult to make up that work

Drop Schedules

The Drop or Rotating schedule can be a traditional or block schedule with classes meeting every day or every other day. The unique aspect of the Drop schedule is that the periods are different every day. Depending on whether a school has a 6, 7, or 8 Period schedule will dictate the number of days in a rotation. On day one, the schedule will start with periods 1–7 and then each day following, the last period will be "dropped" and will then start the next day. Times are excluded from this example in order to show an entire rotation of a 7 Period Drop schedule.

Figure 1.9- Drop Schedule

Day 1	Day 2	Day 3	Day 4	Day 5	Day 6	Day 7
Class	**Class**	**Class**	**Class**	**Class**	**Class**	**Class**
Advisory	Advisory	Advisory	Advisory	Advisory	Advisory	Advisory
Pass	Pass	Pass	Pass	Pass	Pass	Pass
1	7	6	5	4	3	2
Pass	Pass	Pass	Pass	Pass	Pass	Pass
2	1	7	6	5	4	3
Pass	Pass	Pass	Pass	Pass	Pass	Pass
3	2	1	7	6	5	4
Pass	Pass	Pass	Pass	Pass	Pass	Pass
Lunch	Lunch	Lunch	Lunch	Lunch	Lunch	Lunch
Pass	Pass	Pass	Pass	Pass	Pass	Pass
4	3	2	1	7	6	5
Pass	Pass	Pass	Pass	Pass	Pass	Pass
5	4	3	2	1	7	6
Pass	Pass	Pass	Pass	Pass	Pass	Pass
6	5	4	3	2	1	7
Pass	Pass	Pass	Pass	Pass	Pass	Pass
7	6	5	4	3	2	1

Benefits

- Students and teachers see each other at different times of the day

Challenges

- If a school has shared staffing or resources, this will be difficult to execute
- Can be very confusing

Mixed Time Schedules

Mixed Time schedules are very common in elementary schools with larger chunks of time allotted for Reading and Math. In a middle school schedule, this is a less common practice given the demands for time and content. If through the data dive process, schools determine that more time should be allocated to specific subjects, using a Mixed Time schedule is a good idea. I do, however, encourage teams to use caution when creating differences in allotments of time in a middle school schedule. Creating more time for one subject will ultimately take away from others; teams must decide if this is appropriate and what perceptions could develop from such choices.

Figure 1.10- Mixed Time Schedule

Class	Begin	End	Length
Advisory	8:00 AM	8:26 AM	26
Pass	8:26 AM	8:29 AM	3
1	8:29 AM	9:39 AM	70
Pass	9:39 AM	9:42 AM	3
2	9:42 AM	10:42 AM	60
Pass	10:42 AM	10:45 AM	3
3	10:45 AM	11:28 AM	43
Pass	11:28 AM	11:31 AM	3
Lunch	11:31 AM	12:01 PM	30
Pass	12:01 PM	12:04 PM	3
4	12:04 PM	12:47 PM	43
Pass	12:47 PM	12:50 PM	3
5	12:50 PM	1:33 PM	43
Pass	1:33 PM	1:36 PM	3
6	1:36 PM	2:19 PM	43
Pass	2:19 PM	2:22 PM	3
7	2:22 PM	3:05 PM	43

Benefits

- Schools can use this to address additional time that may be needed in specific subject areas
- Teachers can provide intervention during the longer blocks without taking away from other subject areas

Challenges

- Professional development for teachers to effectively use the longer periods of time
- Can create disparities between subject areas
- High school courses will require seat hours that might not be met if they meet in a shortened period

CHAPTER 7: TOP 10 RULES FOR SCHEDULING

This section includes the rules I have developed for scheduling over the course of 20 years. These personal favorites come from working with teachers and staff to create responsive schedules that truly meet the needs of students. You may choose one or all of these to help you in your process.

1. Always let the data drive your decisions! I often see teams that "have an idea" that has nothing to do with the data. Consider your needs and start there. For example, if you have achievement gaps with specific populations, start there.

2. Find a way to allot time for the social part of middle school—not just lunch. Middle school students need time to socialize and be their own unique selves. Create time in the days that allows them space to just be themselves.

3. Allow for flexibility in the schedule so that courses can be created or added throughout the year to address student needs. For example, you may not have a need for reading intervention at the beginning of the year, but at the end of the first semester, you may need to add a course. Give yourself some wiggle room to create that Plan B.

4. Provide teachers with common planning time. This will help facilitate both your teams and PLCs.

5. If you have co-teachers who work well together, help them stay together. Effective co-teaching not only helps special populations, but also helps all the students in the room. Giving time for relationships to develop and helping teacher pairs create synergy will only benefit your students.

6. When creating your schedule, be cognizant of your specialists and their schedules. In addition to those who co-teach, I also include in this category those who deliver Occupational Therapy, Speech Therapy, Physical Therapy, Adaptive Physical Education, behavioral health, anything outside of the typical schedule. Remember that if they are to see all of their students, we must be mindful of their schedule. In this rule, I like to say: measure twice, cut once. Specialists are typically spread over multiple grade levels and subject areas; be sure to look at everything when you create their schedules.

7. Keep equity in mind when you create your teams. Be mindful of where you are scheduling your services and who has the bulk of the responsibility. When schools fully embrace the idea of inclusivity and meeting the needs of all students needs and talents should be spread throughout the schedule.

8. If you have classes that are set solely in the special education setting, also schedule that same teacher to have the co-taught setting of that same class. This practice will help keep your special education teacher up with what is happening in the least restrictive environment.

9. Go old school in your preparation phases. School teams can create the schedule using note cards, a white board with magnets, or programs like my personal favorite, Excel. Electronic scheduling programs may not let you be as responsive as your schedule may require so don't let them limit you. Also be prepared to hand schedule students. Oftentimes, the more responsive the scheduling the more you will have to do manually in your electronic scheduling program.

10. With any schedule, there are probably 100 different ways that schedule could be created. Don't be afraid to split blocks to create classes or adjust schedules by 3–5 minutes to add clubs or extra periods. Be creative and have fun. Through the process you will learn so many things about your school and your priorities. All the data you gather will help strengthen your program and meet the needs of your students. It's a puzzle—have fun completing it!

SECTION 3 REVIEW

Let's review the highlights of Section 3 in order to help complete your scheduling journey. If you have successfully completed the components suggested in Section 3 you will have:

1. Developed your scheduling team.
2. Reviewed priorities and chosen the building blocks for your schedule with budget, change, and professional development in mind.
3. Chosen one or two types of schedules that you think would be a good place for your team to start.

You have arrived! Completing Section 3 means you have successfully made it through both the cultural and technical sides of scheduling.

Conclusion

The master schedule is like an iceberg: so much of what happens with the schedule is below the water line. If you've made it this far, you have sufficiently "dropped your water line" and explored both the cultural and technical aspects of the school schedule and what it takes to truly create a responsive middle school schedule.

In Section 1, we discussed the why behind our schedules. I am hoping that you thoroughly reviewed your vision and mission and created belief statements to help drive your work. It lays the foundation for how you will create your schedule and what it will look like. The exercises in this section may cause some friction as you tease out your priorities; it will be important to create norms to help your meetings operate with efficiency and professionalism.

In Section 2, we explored the how of scheduling by completing what I call the deep data dive and identified what your schedule currently offers and what it may need. The data review process leads you through exploring the true intricacies of your current operations and helps you think through what you both need and want for your reimagined schedule. This section will help your team prioritize what you need in your schedule.

In Section 3, we learned the what of schedules by prioritizing needs and exploring which building blocks will be most beneficial for your school and students. Your team can choose who fills which role and how the process will be carried out. This very important team is tasked with reviewing everything that was collected, creating a plan of communication, and choosing any of the schedule options presented, or even creating their very own.

Throughout this book we explored a full scheduling process and tied it directly to the 18 Characteristics. *The Successful Middle School* helps us identify key components of the middle school concept and how to make them come alive in our schools. This book helps you create the structure to make that happen. Scheduling is a wonderful responsibility to have. The possibilities are endless and the ability to meet the needs of all of your students resides in that structure. You are both the artist and the mathematician when it comes to the schedule and your work of art is waiting for you.

References

Black and Latino Students Shut Out of Advanced Coursework Opportunities. (2020) The Education Trust. https://edtrust.org/press-release/black-and-latino-students-shut-out-of-advanced-coursework-opportunities/

Buffum, A. G., Mattos, M., & Weber, C. (2012). *Pyramid response to intervention: Four essential guiding principles.* Bloomington, IN: Solution Tree Press.

Capper, C. A., & Frattura, E. M. (2009). *Meeting the needs of students of all abilities: How leaders go beyond inclusion.* Thousand Oaks, Calif: Corwin Press.

The Data Wise Project at Harvard Graduate School of Education. Access at: https://datawise.gse.harvard.edu/

Donohoo, J. Hattie, J. Eells, R. *The Power of Collective Efficacy.* ASCD. Access at: https://www.ascd.org/el/articles/the-power-of-collective-efficacy

DuFour, R., Fullan, M., & ebrary, Inc. (2013). *Cultures built to last: Systemic PLCs at work.* Bloomington, Ind: Solution Tree Press.

Dufour, R., Marzano, R. J.,(2011). *Leaders of learning: How district, school, and classroom leaders improve student achievement.* United States: Solution Tree Press.

The Glossary of Education Reform. Access at: https://www.edglossary.org/

Hattie, John. (2014). *Visible Learning + Visible Learning for Teachers.* Corwin Pr.

McCarty, Ann (2010)–doctoral dissertation from Virginia Tech–Professional Development for New Teachers to use Constructivist Pedagogy in the Block Period

Muhammad, Anthony. (2018). *TRANSFORMING SCHOOL CULTURE: How to overcome staff division.* Place of publication not identified: Solution Tree Press.

Steele, J. L., Parker Boudett, K. (2007). *Data Wise in Action: A step-by-step guide to using assessment results to improve teaching and learning.* Harvard Education Press

Reeves, D. B. (2012). *Leading change in your school: How to conquer myths, build commitment, and get results.* Alexandria, Va: Association for Supervision and Curriculum Development.

Rettig, M. D. (2013). *Scheduling Strategies for Middle Schools*. Routledge.

Rettig, M.D. (2002). The Effects of Block Scheduling. AASA. https://www.aasa.org/SchoolAdministratorArticle.aspx?id=14852

Sinek, S. (2013). *Start with why: How great leaders inspire everyone to take action*. Kennett Square, Pa.: Soundview Executive Book Summaries.

What are core beliefs? Center for Clinical Interventions. Access at: https://www.cci.health.wa.gov.au/

Zierer, K., Hattie, J. (2017). *10 mindframes for visible learning–teaching for success*. Routledge.

About the Author

Dr. Ann McCarty Perez is a passionate educator with 24 years of experience working in schools to improve processes and outcomes. She has been a middle school teacher, high school assistant principal, middle school principal, and central office administrator for curriculum, instruction, and assessment. She is well versed in state and federal programming and data-driven decision-making. In her various roles she has implemented curriculum writing and review initiatives, program and process reviews, MTSS and responsive instruction, student behavior modification plans and PBIS; coordinated projects to reduce truancy; increased student achievement and closed gaps; provided services for at-risk students; and collaborated with parents to create a positive school culture. Her experience spans a variety of school settings, including urban, suburban, and rural.

As a presenter and facilitator, Dr. McCarty Perez has helped school leaders with vision and mission, scheduling, equity and courageous leadership, implementation of MTSS, power standards, and using professional learning communities to increase teacher capacity and improve instructional outcomes. As a school and district leader, she has demonstrated a keen ability to close achievement gaps and improve outcomes for all students through continuous improvement efforts and strategic planning. In addition to her work in P–12 education, Dr. McCarty Perez has been an adjunct professor at George Washington University where she worked with aspiring school leaders on instructional supervision.

Her love of scheduling began when she was tasked with completing the schedule in her first middle school assistant principal position. Over the past 18 years, she has worked and studied a wide variety of schedules and is passionate about helping schools develop the schedule that best positions *their* students to succeed.

CPSIA information can be obtained
at www.ICGtesting.com
Printed in the USA
LVHW060541070422
715424LV00002B/5